INTERNATIONAL DEVELOPMENT IN FOCUS

Learning Environments and Learning Achievement in the Russian Federation

How School Infrastructure and Climate Affect Student Success

TIGRAN SHMIS, MARIA USTINOVA, AND DMITRY CHUGUNOV

Contents

Tables

Acknowledgments

This report was prepared by a World Bank team led by Tigran Shmis (senior education specialist, Education Global Practice) and includes contributions from Maria Ustinova (education consultant, Education Global Practice) and Dmitry Chugunov (education economist, Education Global Practice). A team of consultants from the Russian Academy of Education, led by Galina Kovaleva, provided immense support to the team by collecting the data and linking the two data sets used in this study. The team is also grateful to Alexander Bunten and Mikhail Elkin for their support in editing the text. This study would not be possible without the contributions from the principals, teachers, and students who replied to the questions and took the tests.

The work was carried out under the guidance of Andras Horvai (Russia country director), Dorota Nowak (country program coordinator), and Harry Patrinos (practice manager). The publication benefited from comments and discussions with peer reviewers Enrique Alasino (senior education specialist, Education Global Practice), Quentin Wodon (lead economist, Education Global Practice), Kirill Vasiliev (senior education specialist, Education Global Practice), Pedro Cerdan-Infantes (senior economist, Education Global Practice), and Julie Velissaratou (OECD consultant, Effective Learning Environments Group), who provided valuable advice at different stages of this work.

The team is very thankful to the Organisation for Economic Co-operation and Development (OECD) Group of National Experts on Effective Learning Environments and especially to Joanne Caddy, Ria Sandilands, Alastair Blyth, and Julie Velissaratou, who have been excellent partners in this research and beyond it in our work in the Russian Federation and in Europe and Central Asia overall.

About the Authors

Tigran Shmis holds a specialist degree (2001) as a school teacher of computer sciences and economics. He also completed postgraduate study in educational ICTs and holds a PhD (candidate of sciences) degree (2004) from the Russian Academy of Education. Later he completed the MEd (2007) program at the Moscow branch of the University of Manchester on management in education and educational policy. Tigran has worked on educational projects in the Russian Federation, Belarus, Kazakhstan, Kyrgyz Republic, Romania, Serbia, and Peru. Among those projects were the Yakutia Early Childhood Development (ECD) Project, Russian Education Aid for Development (READ), Khanty-Mansyisk ECD infrastructure development technical assistance, Kyrgyz ECD Project, Belarus Education Modernization Project, Serbia ECD Project, and technical Assistance on Safer Schools development project in Peru. He delivered several cooperation programs for the OECD Center for Effective Learning Environments (CELE) and Early Childhood Education and Care (ECEC) networks and UNESCO. Areas of research and professional interests are ECD, innovative learning environments, and international assessment work. Tigran leads work on innovative learning environments, ECD quality initiatives, and capacity building of Russia in international development aid in education.

Maria Ustinova works as a consultant at the World Bank office in Moscow, where she supports various technical assistance and lending projects in the field of education and social protection. She also serves as an associate researcher at the Urban Health Games Research Group, which is a part of the Architecture Department at the Technical University of Darmstadt, Germany. She contributes to research projects investigating how urban planning and design influence human health and well-being, particularly focusing on school learning environments. Additionally, she teaches a course on "Learning Environments Design Foundations" at Moscow City University. Maria holds a double master's degree in international cooperation and urban development from Darmstadt University of Technology, Germany, and Tor Vergata University of Rome, Italy. Prior to joining the Bank, she worked as a consultant for the United Nations Economic Commission for Europe as well as for various projects of the Directorate-General for Education and Culture at the European Commission and the Education, Audiovisual and Culture Executive Agency of the European Union. Her areas of research and professional interest include education facilities design, early childhood development, health promoting design, and participatory practices in education facilities design.

Dmitry Chugunov is an education economist with over seven years of international experience working at the national and international level on education policy and capacity building projects. He has global work experience with development aid agencies in Africa, Europe, and Central Asia and specialized in education policy analysis, impact evaluation (pre- and post-intervention), cost analysis and projection, mobile data collection, student assessment, and workforce and skills development. He has authored or co-authored over 30 analytical reports, articles, and knowledge products in the above areas and is proficient in large dataset management and economic modeling. Dmitry is dedicated to creating evidence-based policy recommendations through high-quality analysis. Dmitry holds a PhD in economics with a specialization in public economics and a master's degree in economics with a specialization in public finance from the National Research University Higher School of Economics in Moscow.

Executive Summary

The design of learning environments and its potential impact on the academic outcomes of pupils is gaining momentum in different countries. According to the Sustainable Development Goal on education, building high-quality education facilities contributes to the achievement of inclusive and equitable education for all. Empirical studies in this area could support the development of evidence-based policies, but they remain few in number.

In 2015 the Russian Federation initiated several federal investment programs to develop school infrastructure. Finding ways to make these investments as efficient as possible remains relevant not only for Russia but also for other countries that allocate significant funding for the construction of education facilities. To understand the relation between physical settings and the learning process, in 2018 the World Bank initiated a study on school infrastructure in Russia.

RESEARCH QUESTION

The World Bank used two instruments to analyze the association between school learning environments and student outcomes: the Organization for Economic Co-operation and Development (OECD) School User Survey (SUS) (OECD 2018) and the Trends in Mathematics and Science Study (TIMSS 2019) pilot in three Russian regions. The study examined the hypothesis that school infrastructure characteristics and the way in which the learning environment is used and arranged might affect learning outcomes as measured by TIMSS. This report discusses the correlations found in the study and identifies the main factors for better education policy.

DATA

This research is based on answers collected from 1,550 students in grade 8, 160 teachers, and 32 school principals. The data include information on the use and characteristics of school infrastructure, student scores on math and science, as well as information on the socioeconomic background of students.

MAIN FINDINGS

The results of the study are discussed across three thematic areas:

- *School infrastructure and its use.* Learning environments remain traditional in most of the schools. Most of the learning takes place in classrooms, and teachers do not use other spaces. Teachers report that rearranging the furniture is easy but that they rarely do so. Lastly, diverse technological equipment is available, but its full capacity is not used.

- *School environment and climate.* The temperature, lighting, quality of air, and noise in classrooms influence students and teachers in Russia. Teachers have fewer issues with the physical characteristics of the building than students; they also express a higher level of satisfaction. Another issue is the level of security in schools, especially regarding outdoor spaces within the school grounds. The users' perception of schools is linked directly with the learning outcomes of students. Teachers and managers agree that better schools help to attract, retain, and keep teachers at work. Lastly, bullying in Russian schools significantly undermines student outcomes, especially among students with low socioeconomic status (SES).

- *Teaching styles.* Diverse teaching styles are in use, as revealed by the questionnaires conducted in Russian schools. Russian teachers do practice team teaching, but rarely. When employed, team teaching and group work have a statistically significant effect on student outcomes, potentially explaining the learning gap of two-thirds of a year as measured by TIMSS. The distribution of teaching methods is an important factor: students with low SES receive less group work and less individual work, even though these methods are effective for students from the bottom 40 percent of SES distribution.

The study confirms that the characteristics of school infrastructure and teaching styles have a relation with learning. Extending the sample to other regions of Russia would yield more statistically significant results and provide additional information to strengthen further research on the design and quality of learning environments.

REFERENCES

OECD (Organisation for Economic Co-operation and Development). 2018. *OECD School User Survey: Improving Learning Space Together.* http://www.oecd.org/education/OECD-School -User-Survey-2018.pdf.

TIMSS (Trends in Mathematics and Science Study). 2019. Retrieved at: http://www.centeroko.ru /timss19/timss2019_info.html.

Abbreviations

ECD	early childhood development
LCD	liquid-crystal display
LEEP	Learning Environments Evaluation Programme
OECD	Organisation for Economic Co-operation and Development
SACERS	School-Age Care Environment Rating Scale
SDG	Sustainable Development Goal
SEN	special educational need
SES	socioeconomic status
SUS	School User Survey
TIMSS	Trends in Mathematics and Science Study

1 Introduction

Over the last eight years, the World Bank has been researching the topic of learning environments in early childhood development (ECD), school, and university settings. The work was financed through various sources, including investment loan project preparation in the Yakutia region of the Russian Federation as well as several reimbursable advisory services activities in the field of ECD and higher education. During these years, the Bank team sought to understand the physical context in which the learning process, as well as the interaction between students and teachers, occurs. The major question that remained unanswered was the reason why investing in the development of learning environments is important and how to make these investments more efficient and compelling.

This report presents a rigorous analysis of the data collected throughout 2018–19 as part of the Organization for Economic Co-operation and Development (OECD) School User Survey (SUS) (OECD 2018) and the Trends in Mathematics and Science Study (TIMSS 2019) piloted in three regions of Russia. This report addresses the findings relevant to national and international researchers and policy makers.

BACKGROUND

At a global level, the development of learning environments is an emerging discipline, which still lacks empirical evidence to show how space is used and how it affects student outcomes and teacher productivity (Blackmore et al. 2011). In 2019 the World Bank published a comprehensive review of research on learning environments from an evidence-based perspective, which found that the number of empirical studies is still scarce and focused mostly on high-income countries (Barrett et al. 2019). The lack of empirical studies on what works in learning environments is worrisome, given the amount of funding spent on school infrastructure globally. Recently, the United Nations introduced new Sustainable Development Goals (SDGs) on education, which include a target and indicator related to the quality of learning environments in education facilities (table 1.1). SDG 4.A indicates that stronger attention is being given to the topic of learning environments and that evidence is being gathered to support better schools around the world.

Global trends show that school systems are changing and that the major driver of change is the agenda of 21st-century learning. The importance of collaboration,

TABLE 1.1 **Sustainable Development Goal on education**

GOAL	INDICATOR
SDG 4.A Build and upgrade education facilities that are child, disability, and gender sensitive and provide safe, nonviolent, inclusive, and effective learning environments for all	SDG 4.A.1 Proportion of schools with access to (a) electricity, (b) the Internet for pedagogical purposes, (c) computers for pedagogical purposes, (d) adapted infrastructure and materials for students with disabilities, (e) basic drinking water, (f) single-sex basic sanitation facilities, and (g) basic handwashing facilities (as per the definitions under the water, sanitation, and hygiene indicator)

Source: United Nations, Sustainable Development Goal 4, https://sustainabledevelopment.un.org/sdg4.
Note: SDG = Sustainable Development Goals.

critical thinking, problem solving, creativity, and other skills is being reflected in changes to teaching practices and learning environments. The most advanced countries in these areas have been successful in innovating and implementing the adjustments to learning environments at the national scale. A recent World Bank study widely supports the argument that flexible, open, safe, and efficient infrastructure does have an impact on learning (Barrett et al. 2019).

Russia has initiated an ambitious infrastructure program to improve learning environments in all schools, provide 6.5 million new places for pupils, and implement a full-time school initiative across the country by 2025 ("Assistance to Create New Places in Public Schools in the Regions of the Russian Federation," Government Decree no. 2145-p, School 2025). Starting in 2017, the Ministry of Education (Instruction) implemented this federal program in the framework of a priority project, Creating Contemporary Learning Environments for Pupils. In 2017, 83 new schools were built in the Russian regions, including 28 schools in rural areas. One year of program implementation has revealed several challenges: (a) the need to improve the regulatory environment related to school design, planning, construction, and maintenance; (b) the need to improve the financing mechanisms of the program, and (c) the need to address the lack of community involvement in designing schools.

Additionally, the Russian government has started to implement a program related to the promotion of digital technologies and online learning in primary and secondary education entitled "Contemporary Digital Learning Environment in the Russian Federation". Focusing on teaching methods, distance learning, and the promotion of massive online open courses (MOOCs), the program is expected to have an impact on conventional spatial arrangements of classrooms and overall school designs in the future. Understanding this impact requires a thorough evaluation of the needs of pupils and teachers regarding the effectiveness and sufficiency of existing learning environments.

The key requirements for school learning environments in Russia are identified in the Federal State Standards of Primary, Basic, and Secondary Education (table 1.2). The standards focus on safety, health, and equal access to education for all pupils. However, the overall characteristics remain very general for all grades.

The Russian experts estimate that the quality and usability of spatial organization in Russian schools are at average levels. For example, based on the School-Age Care Environment Rating Scale (SACERS), schools in Moscow have low scores related to the quality of the following parameters: space and furnishings, time devoted to physical activity, and special needs (for example, the creation of conditions for students with special educational needs). The experts noted a missing connection between the social and pedagogical demands and current design of schools (Ivanova and Vinogradova 2018). The development of design briefs and the design of new buildings often do not consider the needs of the pedagogical community, students, parents, and the municipality. This lack of consideration hinders the development of

TABLE 1.2 **Learning environment requirements in the standards for primary and secondary education in the Russian Federation**

GOAL	PRIMARY EDUCATION: GRADES 1–4	BASIC EDUCATION: GRADES 5–9	SECONDARY EDUCATION (HIGH SCHOOL): GRADES 10–11
Create a unified educational environment and developing social skills	• Create equal opportunities for access to primary education	• Provide access to high-quality basic (general) education	• Create equal opportunities for receiving a high-quality secondary education
Create a comfortable, stimulating learning environment with special requirements for the building, outdoor space, and furniture	• Provide high-quality education • Create conditions for individual child development • Provide an opportunity for barrier-free access for children with special educational needs (SENs) • Ensure safety	• Provide high-quality education • Organize lessons and extracurricular activities • Create conditions for individual child development • Create an opportunity for barrier-free access for children with SENs • Ensure safety	• Provide high-quality education • Organize lessons and extracurricular activities • Create conditions for individual child development • Create an opportunity for barrier-free access for children with SENs • Create conditions for group, individual, project, and creative work • Ensure safety

Source: Russian Federal Standards of Primary and Secondary Education.

contemporary learning environments and seriously affects the quality and comfort of modern schools.

At the same time, international best practices and the growing pool of scientific evidence suggest that only a holistic approach to school design and planning can guarantee a high quality of education facilities, high quality of education provided, and well-being of pupils and teachers (Barrett et al. 2019). Several key parameters are important to consider at all stages of design, implementation, operation, and supervision of future education infrastructure projects (figure 1.1):

- *Accessible.* The school facility should be accessible to both pupils and teachers. Schools with effective access have the following characteristics: they are locally distributed to maintain reasonable travel distances to school, are relatively small, have relatively small classes and relatively low density of classroom occupancy, are used for a school day of reasonable length, and have optimal scheduling to maximize educational benefits (Leithwood and Jantzi 2009).

- *Well-built.* The physical quality of the built environment should ensure the safety and good health of the users. The school's buildings should be ready to withstand natural disasters, provide basic services and opportunities for outside play, and have good indoor environmental quality. These factors may contribute positively to pupils attending and remaining healthy in school and help to retain teachers (Barrett et al. 2015; Buckley, Schneider, and Shang 2004; Mendell and Heath 2005; OECD 2017b).

- *Child-centered.* Physical characteristics of the built environment should positively affect and stimulate the educational progress of pupils. The design should take into account the needs of the children and their age as well as local climatic and cultural conditions and should guarantee good "natural" parameters such as lighting, air quality, temperature control, acoustics, and links to nature, color, and visual complexity (Barrett et al. 2015). The learning spaces should be easy to navigate, be well connected, and provide additional learning opportunities.

- *Synergetic.* The built environment should fit with the pedagogy provided by the school and with the daily life and needs of the surrounding community. The main

FIGURE 1.1

Learning environments for better educational outcomes

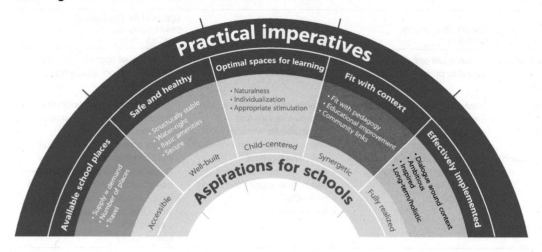

Source: Barrett et al. 2019.

users of the school—especially the school principal—should participate in the design process (OECD 2013; Realdania 2010; Seydel 2017).

• *Fully realized*. Strong attention to these factors may help to improve the efficiency of the resources invested in school infrastructure projects and could lead to more effective cooperation between stakeholders involved in the development and operation of school infrastructure.

RESEARCH QUESTIONS AND METHODOLOGY OF THE STUDY

Two instruments were used to analyze the relation between school learning environments and student outcomes: the OECD School User Survey and the Trends in Mathematics and Science Study pilot in Russian regions.

School characteristics and perceptions

Globally, only a few research groups are focusing on the connectedness of learning environments and learning outcomes. They include the OECD Group of National Experts on Effective Learning Environments and the Australian Innovative Learning Environments Research Group at the University of Melbourne. While the OECD's research focuses on teaching and learning interactions, the Australian research focuses on the architectural layout of schools. The Australian research is difficult to apply in Russia because schools with open plans are rare. The suggested instrument covers mostly the *well-built*, *child-centered*, and *synergetic* areas of the proposed framework.

The SUS is a survey tool for analyzing school characteristics collected from students, teachers, and school leaders or principals. The questionnaires can be used to collect and triangulate evidence on the actual use of learning spaces as well as to solicit user perspectives. The SUS was developed by the OECD Learning Environments Evaluation Programme (LEEP).[1]

This study focuses on the broader concept of learning spaces, which includes physical characteristics, use of learning spaces, security, and cultural perspectives.

FIGURE 1.2

Structure of the OECD School User Survey questionnaires

	Student questionnaire	Teacher questionnaire	School questionnaire
Section 1	About you	About you	About you
Section 2	Spaces you use	About your school	The physical environment of the school
Section 3	Comfort	Spaces you see	Technology at the school
Section 4	Safety and well-being	Comfort	Overall satisfaction
Section 5	Overall satisfaction	Technology	
Section 6		Arrangement of the space	
Section 7		Space for administrative work and class preparation	
Section 8		Overall satisfaction	

Source: OECD 2017a.
Note: Color coding shows the cross-cutting blocks.

It therefore uses the SUS, which captures both physical and nonphysical characteristics of learning environments (see figure 1.2).

This report does not use the latest version of the questionnaires; an up-to-date version is available on the Internet.[2]

Student performance

To measure student performance, the World Bank used the pilot trial of TIMSS 2019. The pilot trial tested the TIMMS 2019 questions in order to improve the methodology. It also produced local results for learning outcomes of students in mathematics and science. The outcome results are not weighed and scaled on the international scale, which is usually from 0 to 1,000 points. This does not mean that the results are invalid; it does mean that the TIMSS pilot results in this analysis cannot be used for international comparisons. However, they can be used for analyzing Russian results in three pilot regions. In the pilot sample, the scores are distributed from 0 to 100.

The pilot testing took place in three Russian regions and included 1,550 students in grade 8, 160 teachers, and 32 school principals. The analysis includes student performance scores in mathematics and science. Every student completed the full set of tasks in math and science and received a score in each category as well as generalized TIMSS scores.

Data collection and sample

Every student who took the TIMSS in the sampled schools filled out the SUS student questionnaire. Teachers of the students who participated in the TIMSS

FIGURE 1.3

Data connectivity for the study

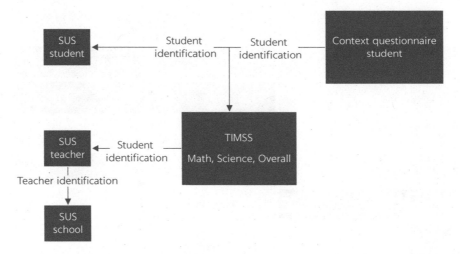

Source: World Bank estimates based on the Trends in Mathematics and Science Study (TIMSS 2019) and OECD School User Survey (SUS) (OECD 2018) data.
Note: SUS = OECD School User Survey, TIMSS = Trends in Mathematics and Science Study.

testing from the sampled schools and classes filled out the SUS teacher questionnaire. School principals of the sampled schools filled out the SUS school questionnaire (see figure 1.3). The procedure in the schools lasted two days. During the first day, students, teachers, and principals participated in the TIMSS testing, and the next day they completed the SUS forms. The questionnaires were delivered in paper and pencil form.

The sample includes mostly urban schools, located in the central and northwest administrative districts of the country in three pilot regions. The sample does not include different types of schools (for example, private, specialized); thus, it does not allow for analyzing the potential disparities between those types of schools and between the regions of Russia.

Preliminary hypotheses associated with the School User Survey suggest that school infrastructure characteristics and how the learning environment is used and arranged might affect learning outcomes as measured by TIMSS. The study sought to answer the following questions:

1. How do school users perceive and use the school learning environment in Russia?

2. How does the school learning environment affect student achievements?

3. How does the school learning environment affect the development of 21st-century skills?

4. What factors may be considered for better education policy related to school learning environments?

NOTES

1. For more information about SUS and LEEP see http://www.oecd.org/education/effective
-learning-environments/.
2. For more information on the survey see http://www.oecd.org/education/OECD-School-User
-Survey-2018.pdf.

REFERENCES

Barrett, Peter, Fay Davies, Yufan Zhang, and Lucinda Barrett. 2015. "The Impact of Classroom Design on Pupils' Learning: Final Results of a Holistic, Multi-Level Analysis." *Building and Environment* 89 (July): 118–33.

Barrett, Peter, Alberto Treves, Tigran Shmis, Diego Ambasz, and Maria Ustinova. 2019. *The Impact of School Infrastructure on Learning: A Synthesis of the Evidence.* International Development in Focus. Washington, DC: World Bank. https://openknowledge.worldbank.org/handle/10986/30920.

Blackmore, Joe, Debra Bateman, Joanne O'Mara, and Jill Loughlin. 2011. *The Connections between Learning Spaces and Learning Outcomes: People and Learning Places?* Victoria: Centre for Research in Educational Futures and Innovation, Faculty of Arts and Education, Deakin University.

Buckley, Jack, Mark Schneider, and Yi Shang. 2004. *The Effects of School Facility Quality on Teacher Retention in Urban School Districts.* Washington, DC: National Clearinghouse for Educational Facilities.

Ivanova, Elena, and Irina Vinogradova. 2018. "Scales SACERS: Results of the Study of the Educational Environment of Moscow Schools." *European Journal of Contemporary Education* 7 (3): 498–510. doi:10.13187/ejced.2018.3.498.

Leithwood, Kenneth, and Doris Jantzi. 2009. "A Review of Empirical Evidence about School Size Effects: A Policy Perspective." *Review of Research in Education* 79 (1): 464–90.

Mendell, J. Mark, and Garvin A. Heath. 2005. "Do Indoor Pollutants and Thermal Conditions in Schools Influence Student Performance? A Critical Review of the Literature." *Indoor Air* 15 (1): 27–52.

OECD (Organisation for Economic Co-operation and Development). 2013. *Innovative Learning Environments.* Educational Research and Innovation. Paris: OECD.

———. 2017a. "LEEP Field Trial Implementation Report." EDU/EDPC/GNEELE(2017)5, Group of National Experts on Effective Learning Environments, Directorate for Education and Skills, Education Policy Committee, OECD, Paris. http://www.oecd.org/education/LEEP-FIELD-TRIAL-IMPLEMENTATION-REPORT.pdf.

———. 2017b. *Protecting Students and Schools From Earthquakes: The Seven OECD Principles For School Seismic Safety.* Paris: OECD.

———. 2018. *OECD School User Survey: Improving Learning Space Together.* http://www.oecd.org/education/OECD-School-User-Survey-2018.pdf.

Realdania. 2010. "МОДЕЛЬНАЯ ПРОГРАММА ДЛЯ ОБЩЕОБРАЗОВАТЕЛЬНЫХ ШКОЛАгентство [Danish Model Program for Schools]." Realdania, Copenhagen. http://documents.worldbank.org/curated/en/734251533070308219/pdf/Danish-Modelprogram-for-Schools-RUS.pdf.

Seydel, Otto. 2017. "Reflections on the Relationship between Schools and the City." In *Education, Space, and Urban Planning: Education as a Component of the City,* edited by Angela Million, Anna J. Heinrich, and Thomas Coelen, 19–29. Cham, Switzerland: Springer International.

TIMSS (Trends in Mathematics and Science Study). 2019. Retrieved at: http://www.centeroko.ru/timss19/timss2019_info.html.

2 Results and Discussion

The results presented in this section are structured based on several criteria derived from the data and design of the questionnaires. The first part analyzes *physical environment and its use* by looking at the Organisation for Economic Co-operation and Development (OECD) School User Survey (SUS) questionnaires. The second part discusses *school environment and climate,* presenting perceptions and safety and analyzing bullying in different dimensions, including the impact on learning outcomes. The third part focuses on *teaching practices and learning outcomes,* analyzing the approaches to teaching and links to the academic performance of students.

Although this study uses two linked data sets, the link between learning outcomes and school characteristics is a correlation, not a causality. The forthcoming larger data sets with country-representative sampling will help to make a stronger argument for the causality of the findings.

THE PHYSICAL ENVIRONMENT AND ITS USE

Major findings: *Learning environments are traditional in most of the reviewed schools, and the majority of learning takes place in classrooms. In most cases, teachers do not use spaces beyond classrooms. Although moving furniture is possible and easy—as reported by teachers—it rarely takes place. Lastly, schools have an array of technological equipment, but technology is reportedly used infrequently.*

The types of spaces, their spatial organization, their allocation, and the frequency of use by students and teachers provide valuable information about the organization and practices of teaching and learning. This information, in turn, can indicate how the spaces might shape teaching and learning processes, affect health and well-being, and shape learning and social outcomes.

The majority of teachers surveyed (70 percent) use only one classroom for teaching. Teachers who use only one classroom are five years older than their colleagues who use multiple places for their classes: 51 years old compared with 46 years old. The difference in age is statistically significant at the 0.05 percent level. All of the teachers surveyed confirmed that there is only one teacher in the classroom during lessons.

FIGURE 2.1

Frequency of use of spaces by students and teachers in a typical week

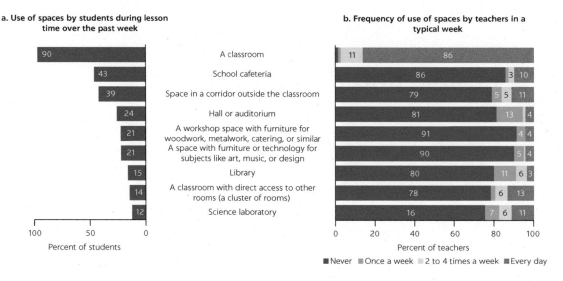

Source: World Bank estimates based on OECD School User Survey (SUS) (OECD 2018) data.

Regarding the types of spaces and their frequency of use (figure 2.1), both teachers and students reported that in a typical week they only use their classrooms during lesson time. The vast majority (97 percent) of teachers teach in classrooms assigned to them at least two to four times a week, and 90 percent of students use a single classroom during lesson time.

Students use the school cafeteria and corridors outside the classroom most frequently for lesson time during a typical week. However, only 13 percent of teachers reported using the school cafeteria for teaching purposes at least two to four times in a typical week, while 43 percent of students reported using the cafeteria during lesson times over the past week. In addition, 21 percent of teachers reported using the space in a corridor outside the classroom in a typical week, compared with 39 percent of students over the past week.

Research suggests that flexible spaces can encourage more effective teaching (Anderson-Butcher et al. 2010; Oblinger and Lippincott 2006), team teaching, better planning, use of more diverse pedagogies, and focus on personalized learning. Flexible spaces can also encourage students to be self-reliant learners capable of working in groups (Dekker, Elshout-Mohr, and Wood 2006; Fielding 2006).

The physical learning environment in Russian schools may be used to suit a variety of instructional methods and, in some cases, may be conducive particularly to methods relevant for 21st-century teaching and learning, such as group work. Research shows that group work can lead to more active and sustained engagement, connectedness, and higher-order inferential joint reasoning among students (Blatchford et al. 2006).

Regarding the flexibility and adjustability of spaces—the ease of arranging and rearranging furniture—the majority (79 percent) of teachers agreed that it is easy to rearrange the furniture (figure 2.2). Only 21 percent of teachers disagreed with this statement. The majority (83 percent) of teachers also agreed that there is enough space to arrange furniture in different ways, and more than half (60 percent) agreed that the furniture can be moved easily during lesson time.

FIGURE 2.2

Teachers' agreement with statements about moving furniture

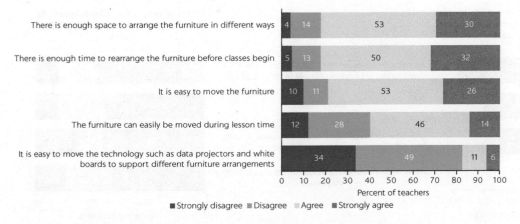

Source: World Bank estimates based on OECD School User Survey (SUS) (OECD 2018) data.

FIGURE 2.3

Frequency of spatial arrangements by teachers

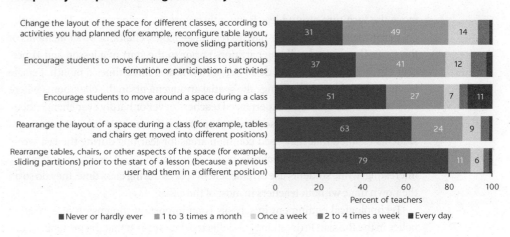

Source: World Bank estimates based on OECD School User Survey (SUS) (OECD 2018) data.

However, 93 percent of teachers said that it is difficult to move the technology equipment, such as liquid-crystal display (LCD) projectors and whiteboards, to support different furniture arrangements. Only 17 percent reported that they find it easy—49 percent disagreed and 34 percent strongly disagreed.

The majority (82 percent) of teachers said that there is enough time to rearrange the furniture before classes begin. For this reason, on average, teachers do not encourage students to move around a space during a class or to move the furniture to suit group work (figure 2.3). Only 4 percent of teachers said that they encourage students to move around a space during a class at least two to four times a week, whereas a little less than a third (27 percent) said that they encourage students to do so one to three times a month.

More than a third (41 percent) of teachers also encourage students to move furniture during class one to three times a month to suit group formation or participation in activities, while 12 percent do so at least once a week. Teachers by themselves

FIGURE 2.4

Use of external (outside) spaces by students and teachers

a. Use of external or outside spaces by students during class times over the last week

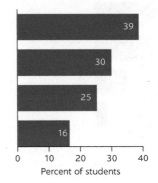

An external (outside) hard ball court, sports court, hard paved area not accessible from a classroom

Sports field

An external (outside) classroom or space, usually with seating and directly accessible from a classroom

Grassy area (not a sports field) not accessible from a classroom

b. Use of external or outside spaces by teachers during class times over the last week

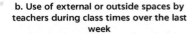
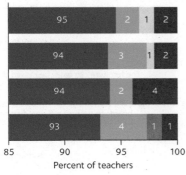

Percent of students

Percent of teachers

■ Never or hardly ever   ■ 1 to 3 times a month
■ 2 to 4 times a week   ■ Once a week
■ Every day

Source: World Bank estimates based on OECD School User Survey (SUS) (OECD 2018) data.

move the furniture around less frequently before or during a class. The majority (79 percent) of teachers never have to rearrange tables, chairs, or other elements of the space (for example, sliding partitions) prior to the start of a lesson and 11 percent of teachers only have to do so between one and three times a month. Female teachers more frequently change the spatial arrangements in the classrooms where they teach. Older and more experienced teachers never or hardly ever change them.

Students and teachers use external spaces differently. While 39 percent of students claimed that they used common areas for learning during the last week, 95 percent of teachers said that they never do it (figure 2.4). The conclusion is very interesting: while students use diverse school spaces during class time, they do so on their own time, without teachers in most of the cases.

Technological equipment in schools is an important dimension of education policy in the Russian Federation. The collected data suggest that the presence of different types of technology is uneven within schools and that the use of technology still lags behind its availability. Still, whiteboards (interactive boards) are not available to teachers, and wireless Internet and tablets are never used in 43 percent and 96 percent of cases, respectively. Projectors are the most commonly used technology (72 percent), compared with 34 percent for laptops and 49 percent for the Internet (figure 2.5).

The following summarizes the findings regarding the physical environment of schools and its use:

• Diverse use of space by teachers: low

• Rearrangement of space and ease of doing so: high

• Use of external spaces: low

• Diversity of technology: high

• Frequency of technology use: low.

FIGURE 2.5

Availability of technologies and frequency of use

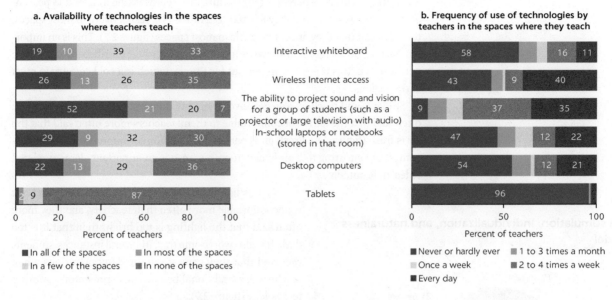

a. Availability of technologies in the spaces where teachers teach

b. Frequency of use of technologies by teachers in the spaces where they teach

Source: World Bank estimates based on OECD School User Survey (SUS) (OECD 2018) data.

SCHOOL ENVIRONMENT AND CLIMATE

Major findings: *The conditions in Russian schools provide diverse experiences for users. The users' perceptions of temperature, lighting, quality of air, and noise influence both students and teachers in Russia. Teachers have fewer issues with the physical characteristics of the building than students and have a higher level of satisfaction. The issues with lighting pertain more often to lighting that is too bright rather than to lighting that is too dim. Security is an issue, especially for schools with external amenities. The users' perception of schools has a direct link with the learning outcomes of students. Teachers and school managers agree that better schools help to attract, retain, and keep teachers at work. Lastly, bullying significantly undermines student outcomes, especially among students with low socioeconomic status (SES).*

This section addresses the *physical* and *nonphysical* characteristics of learning environments in Russian schools. The physical characteristics include the perception of students and teachers regarding temperature, air quality, and lighting in the schools. The nonphysical aspects include the arrangement of spaces, the perception of users regarding the arrangement, and security issues of the schools. Research has shown a positive relationship between the physical condition of a school and student learning that eventually results in better life outcomes for those students (Barrett et al. 2019). A study conducted at the University of Salford in the United Kingdom (Barrett et al. 2015) found that differences in the physical characteristics of classrooms accounted for almost half of 16 percent of variations in learning progress between students over just one year in primary school. The most influential factors were environmental (such as light, temperature, and air quality), followed by classroom design, including flexibility, students' sense of ownership, and surrounding color (figure 2.6).

Physical characteristics

Students and teachers perceive temperature differently. While in 15 and 13 percent of cases students said that they feel too cold or too hot, respectively, in most spaces, teachers said that they are comfortable in most spaces (figure 2.7). This is an important factor, and, as research shows, temperature is a strong contributor to academic performance. It is especially important for Russia, which is a cold country in most of the regions.

Students and teachers also perceive air quality differently. While students more often said that the air is not comfortable to them, teachers more often said that the air is fresh (figure 2.8). Fresh air is part of the equation for improved learning outcomes, and ensuring that air in classrooms is fresh is an important element related to learning outcomes.

As far as lighting is concerned, students said that light is uncomfortable more often than teachers, and they more often said that the lighting is too bright than that it is too dark. It is also worrisome that, in several instances, students reported that they cannot see the demonstrations when teachers use traditional boards, LCD projectors, or other technology (figure 2.9).

While the trinity of physical characteristics (temperature, air quality, and natural light) has been identified as significant for the United Kingdom, our study suggests the need to consider other characteristics of learning spaces. Auditory comfort is important for students to be able to learn better and understand what teachers say. Students said that they can hear the teacher and peers well in most cases, but they are more often disturbed by external noise (figure 2.10).

Students who experience visual and auditory difficulties in the classroom said that they feel hot or cold in most places and score on average one to two test points lower on both math and science assessments (figure 2.11). The difference may seem minor; however, together with other factors that influence learning (for example, teaching), the relation between the school environment and learning is substantial.

FIGURE 2.6

The stimulation, individualization, and naturalness model

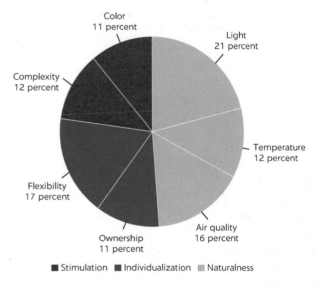

Source: Barrett et al. 2015.
Note: Figure shows the contribution of each classroom measure.

FIGURE 2.7

Temperature felt by students and teachers when it is cold outside

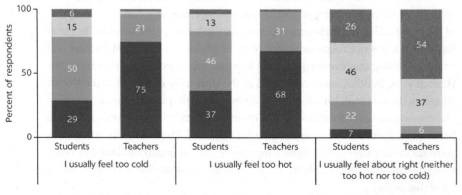

Source: World Bank estimates based on OECD School User Survey (SUS) (OECD 2018) data.

FIGURE 2.8

Air quality felt by students and teachers in spaces where lessons or study takes place

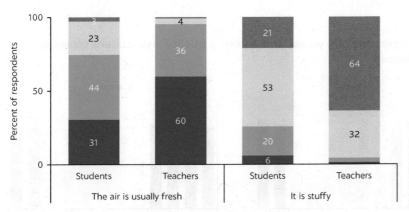

Source: World Bank estimates based on OECD School User Survey (SUS) (OECD 2018) data.

FIGURE 2.9

Perceived visual quality of natural light by students and teachers in the learning spaces when it is daylight outside

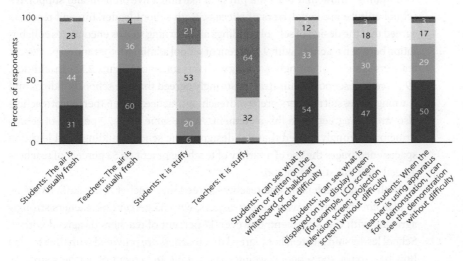

Source: World Bank estimates based on OECD Student User Survey (SUS) (OECD 2018) data.
Note: LCD = liquid-crystal display.

FIGURE 2.10

Perceived auditory quality by students and teacher in learning spaces

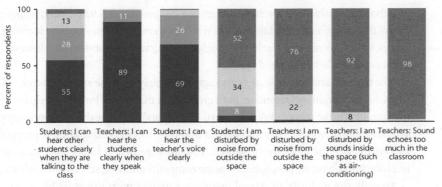

Source: World Bank estimates based on OECD School User Survey (SUS) (OECD 2018) data.

FIGURE 2.11

Perceived temperature, air, visual, and auditory quality and student scores in math and science

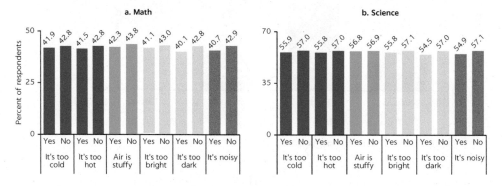

Source: World Bank estimates based on OECD School User Survey (SUS) (OECD 2018) data.

School culture and user perceptions

The findings show that both the physical learning environment and supportive school culture are key drivers of success. Both school leadership and teachers agreed that the design of school buildings and learning spaces encourages collaboration between teachers, with 93 percent of school administrators and 86 percent of teachers agreeing or strongly agreeing with this statement (figure 2.12). In addition, 69 percent of school administrators strongly agreed that the school buildings and learning spaces suit teachers' preferred teaching practice, while 63 percent of teachers also strongly agreed with this statement. At the same time, 70 percent of school principals strongly agreed that the design of the school buildings and learning spaces encourages the use of a variety of teaching practices; 53 percent of teachers agreed with this statement too.

Both school leadership and teachers agreed that teachers have sufficient time to plan collaboratively with other teachers, with 35 percent of teachers strongly agreeing with this statement; however, 17 percent of teachers disagreed with it. School leadership and teachers agreed that teachers are provided with time to plan how best to use the school learning spaces, with 46 percent of teachers strongly agreeing with this statement; however, 10 percent either disagreed or strongly disagreed with it.

The majority of school leaders and teachers (86 percent and 82 percent, respectively) agreed or agreed strongly that school leaders encourage teachers to experiment with different ways of using the learning spaces. However, 15 percent of teachers and 14 percent of school administrators disagreed with it.

School leadership and teachers also agreed (90 percent and 92 percent, respectively) that the school schedule enables teachers to make the most of the learning spaces, with 42 percent of teachers strongly agreeing with this statement. However, 7 percent of teachers disagreed with it.

The teachers and school leaders also agreed strongly with the statements related to teacher attraction and retention. Both groups said that school buildings help to attract teachers to the schools, keep them in their jobs, and stimulate them to stay longer on the school premises. They also agreed that the school building attracts parents looking to place their children in school. The last statement is important given the level of school financing per capita and some competition among schools for students.

Overall, the majority of school users are satisfied with the available school spaces: 87 percent of teachers, 78 percent of students, and 75 percent of school leadership (figure 2.13). However, the difference in satisfaction between teachers and

FIGURE 2.12

School leadership and culture

a. The extent to which schools administators agree or disagree with the following statements about their school's leadership and learning environment

b. The extent to which teachers agree or disagree with the following statements about their school's leadership and learning environment

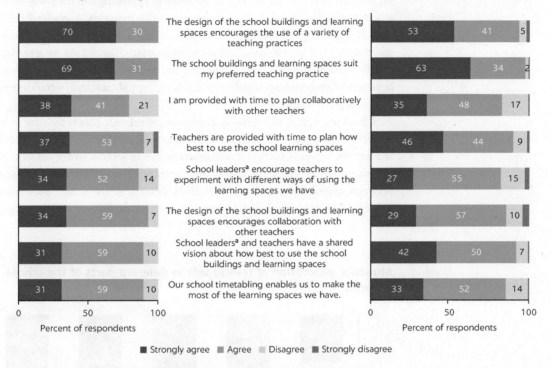

a: 70, 30 / b: 53, 41, 5	The design of the school buildings and learning spaces encourages the use of a variety of teaching practices
a: 69, 31 / b: 63, 34, 2	The school buildings and learning spaces suit my preferred teaching practice
a: 38, 41, 21 / b: 35, 48, 17	I am provided with time to plan collaboratively with other teachers
a: 37, 53, 7 / b: 46, 44, 9	Teachers are provided with time to plan how best to use the school learning spaces
a: 34, 52, 14 / b: 27, 55, 15	School leadersª encourage teachers to experiment with different ways of using the learning spaces we have
a: 34, 59, 7 / b: 29, 57, 10	The design of the school buildings and learning spaces encourages collaboration with other teachers
a: 31, 59, 10 / b: 42, 50, 7	School leadersª and teachers have a shared vision about how best to use the school buildings and learning spaces
a: 31, 59, 10 / b: 33, 52, 14	Our school timetabling enables us to make the most of the learning spaces we have.

Percent of respondents   Percent of respondents

■ Strongly agree ■ Agree ■ Disagree ■ Strongly disagree

Source: World Bank estimates based on OECD School User Survey (SUS) (OECD 2018) data.
a. School leaders include the school principal, deputy principal, and heads of department.

FIGURE 2.13

Average satisfaction with school spaces

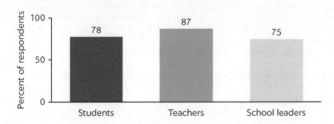

Students: 78   Teachers: 87   School leaders: 75

Source: World Bank estimates based on OECD School User Survey (SUS) (OECD 2018) data.

students is almost 10 percent. Overall, the analysis shows that students more often feel discomfort about lighting, temperature, and noise. This discomfort may explain why their overall satisfaction is lower than that of teachers. The study does not go into the classrooms per se; however, it is possible that the difference in hearing and visual comfort can be explained partly by the classroom seating arrangements. While teachers usually benefit from central positioning, some students sit in areas with less light or more noise than other areas of the room.

School environment index

The school environment index is constructed employing principal component analysis on five variables. The index components are student responses on a scale from 1 ("disagree a lot") to 4 ("agree a lot") to the following statements: (a) "I like being in school," (b) "I feel safe in school," (c) "I feel that I belong to this school," (d) "My teachers are fair to me," and (e) "I am proud to study in my school" (figure 2.14).

The school environment index shows the composite of different inputs. The review also identifies the gender-based differences in school perception. Boys and girls have significantly different perceptions of the sense of belonging and the joy of being in school. Boys said that they feel less belonging and joy than girls. A smaller difference but still statistically significant is the sense of safety felt by boys and girls; again, boys said that they feel less safe on school premises than girls (figure 2.15). An area of similarity is in the fairness of teachers to students and pride in their schools. The difference in the school environment index between girls and boys is statistically significant at the 0.01 percent confidence level.

School perception and learning outcomes are related. This is the case in both subjects of the Trends in International Mathematics and Science Study (TIMSS). Student test scores in math and science are higher in schools where students have a positive perception of the school environment. The difference in test scores between schools in the top and bottom 20 percent of the school environment index is 3.5 points in math and 2.1 points in science, which is equivalent to a gap of

FIGURE 2.14

Students' perception of feeling safe in different parts of the school grounds

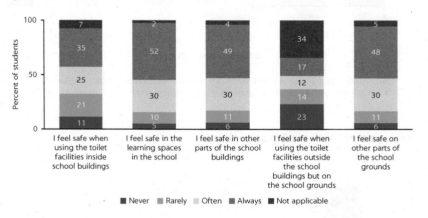

Source: World Bank estimates based on OECD School User Survey (SUS) (OECD 2018) data.

FIGURE 2.15

Components of the school environment index, by gender

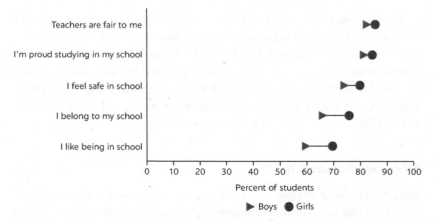

Source: World Bank estimates based on OECD School User Survey (SUS) (OECD 2018) data.

FIGURE 2.16

Student scores, by school environment index quintiles

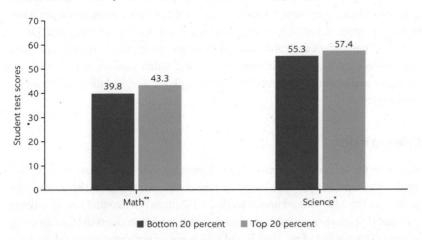

Source: World Bank estimates based on OECD School User Survey (SUS) (OECD 2018) data.
** Statistically significant at 0.05 percent confidence level; * Statistically significant at 0.1 percent confidence level.

FIGURE 2.17

Student motivation and test scores

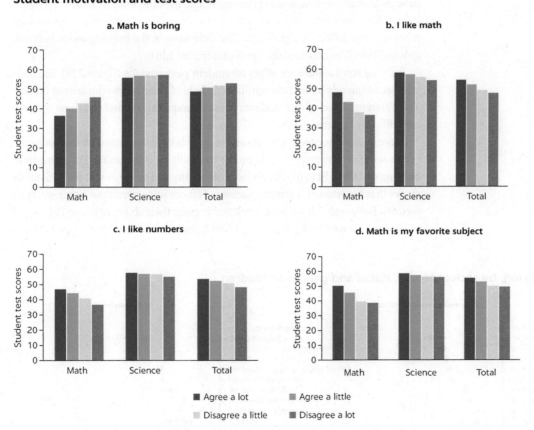

Source: World Bank estimates based on OECD School User Survey (SUS) (OECD 2018) data.

two-thirds of a year of schooling (figure 2.16).[1] This significant gap can be addressed by several measures, including better learning environments.

Student motivation is another area affecting performance. As confirmed in the Programme for International Student Assessment (PISA) 2015 data (World Bank 2018), motivated students can overcome income inequality and highly motivated students from the bottom quintile of the income distribution can achieve the performance on PISA of poorly motivated students from the top quintile. The TIMSS data support this claim. Students saying that they like math and numbers—saying that math is not boring—score significantly higher than students who do not like math (figure 2.17).

School perception and motivation of students can improve learning outcomes and create significant gains in student learning. Other characteristics of school buildings and learning environments can also play a role, including bullying and teaching styles.

Bullying index

Similar to the school environment index, a bullying index was created using principal component analysis. The index has nine components—student responses on a scale from 1 to 3 (3 = at least once a week; 2 = 1–2 times per month; 1 = several times per year; 0 = never)—responding to the statement, "Other students did the following to me": (a) made fun of my clothes; (b) said mean things about me; (c) shared my secrets with others; (d) refused to talk with me; (e) spread embarrassing information about me (including photos), (f) threatened me; (g) hurt me; (h) excluded me from groups including online; or (i) damaged my belongings on purpose.

According to the results of the analysis, more bullying occurs between boys than girls, including violent acts and verbal abuse, and the difference is statistically significant. Girls more often share each other's secrets or refuse to talk than boys, and the difference is statistically significant. The difference in the bullying index between girls and boys is not statistically significant (figure 2.18).

Bullying has a significant effect on student performance (figure 2.19). Students who are frequently bullied are significantly behind their peers who are not bullied. The difference in scores for students who are frequently bullied and those who are not bullied is 6 points.

More bullying occurs (higher index) in schools with students with low socioeconomic status or background.[2] The problem of bullying is important. For a long time, bullying was thought to be only an issue of security and safety in schools. This study shows that the issue of learning outcomes is more important than either safety or security. Bullying holds students back and impairs their ability to learn. The SES of students has a role in the frequency of bullying as well. The distribution between

FIGURE 2.18

Prevalence of bullying, by socioeconomic status and gender of children

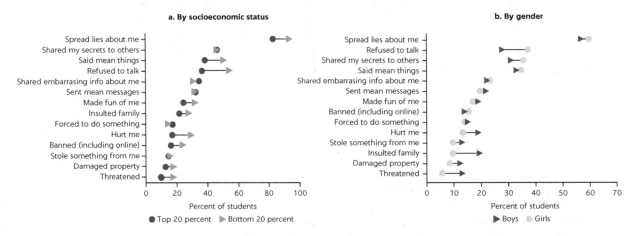

a. By socioeconomic status

b. By gender

● Top 20 percent ▶ Bottom 20 percent

▶ Boys ● Girls

Source: World Bank estimates based on Trends in International Mathematics and Science Study (TIMSS 2019) and OECD School User Survey (SUS) (OECD 2018) data.

FIGURE 2.19

Bullying and learning outcomes

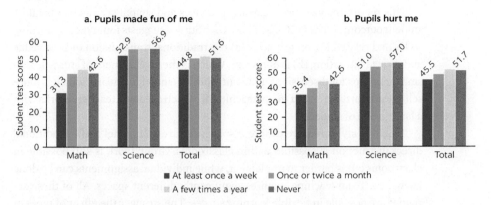

Source: World Bank estimates based on Trends in International Mathematics and Science Study (TIMSS 2019) and OECD School User Survey (SUS) (OECD 2018) data.

FIGURE 2.20

Role of bullying in student performance and its connection to socioeconomic status of students

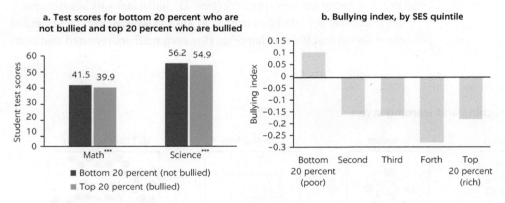

Source: World Bank estimates based on Trends in International Mathematics and Science Study (TIMSS 2019) and OECD School User Survey (SUS) (OECD 2018) data.
Note: SES = socioeconomic status.
*** Key areas of school curricula for TIMSS assessment.

quintiles shows that the maximum amount of bullying happens in the bottom 20 percent of the SES distribution (figure 2.20).

The findings of this section have several policy implications. The issue of bullying is a multidimensional problem related to safety and security, learning outcomes, and equity. Tackling it can help to solve many educational problems, and targeting the effort toward students in the bottom 20 percent of SES is crucially important.

TEACHING PRACTICES AND LEARNING OUTCOMES

Major findings: *The way in which teaching and learning happens is important. The diversity of layouts used, as reported in responses to the SUS questionnaire administered in Russian schools, is surprising. Teachers team teach, though rarely. The teaching approaches used affect student learning outcomes. Team teaching and group work have a statistically significant effect on student outcomes, potentially explaining the two-thirds of a year learning gap reported in TIMSS. The equity in the distribution of teaching methods is also important. While teachers provide group and individual work* *less often to students of low SES, these methods are found to be effective for students from the bottom 40 percent of SES distribution.*

This report analyzes how learning practices and spatial arrangements affect student outcomes. The OECD's School User Survey suggests four types of learning styles and related learning spaces: (a) the traditional transmission of knowledge and direct instruction; (b) group work, which is the arrangement of students into smaller groups for discussions and joint work; (c) individual work, which is more self-paced learning; and (d) team teaching, in which a team of teachers works with a large group of students.

Teaching styles require different spaces (figure 2.21, panel a–d). Traditional direct instruction is possible within classrooms. Group work is still possible in classrooms but is harder to implement, while individual assignments can be done anywhere. Team teaching requires significantly different spaces. All of these activities are possible in flexible learning spaces. The stronger the effect of types of innovative teaching and learning, the stronger the argument for implementation support.

The traditional form of teaching prevails in Russian schools. In the schools sampled for this study, 95 percent of teachers said that they use direct instruction every day or at least two to four times per week (table 2.1). Individual work is also common.

Team teaching is a rare phenomenon in Russian schools, with 68 percent of teachers saying that it never happens. However, teachers reported that team

FIGURE 2.21

Types of teaching and learning styles

a. Presentation	b. Group	c. Individual	d. Team teaching
			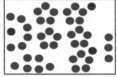
Layouts that support explict instruction or presentation to the whole group	Layouts that support approaches where students are required to collaborate and work in small groups to share ideas and help each other	Layouts that support approaches where students work independently to write, read, research, think, and reflect	Layouts that support approaches where two or more teachers work collaboratively with groups of students sharing the same space

● Teacher ● Pupils

Source: Based on OECD School User Survey (SUS) (OECD 2018) data.

TABLE 2.1 Share of teachers using teaching styles, by frequency

TEACHING STYLE	NEVER	1–3 TIMES PER MONTH	1 PER WEEK	2–4 PER WEEK	EVERY DAY	MISSING
Direct instruction (presentation)	0.65	1.95	2.6	20.78	73.38	0.65
Small group instruction	2.6	31.17	28.57	27.92	6.49	3.25
Individual	3.9	14.29	20.13	24.68	36.36	0.65
Team teaching	68.18	16.88	2.6	1.95	5.19	5.19

Source: World Bank estimates based on OECD School User Survey (SUS) (OECD 2018) data.

teaching occurs between one and three times a month in almost 17 percent of cases and every day in 5 percent of cases. These data suggest that the practices exist, and deeper analysis of those practices may reveal more information about how teachers collaborate and how they use learning spaces. Group work is another rarely used practice. Group work takes place at different levels of intensity, but not every day.

The analysis also shows that more experienced and senior teachers use small group instruction and individual learning approaches more often than inexperienced teachers. Results of a regression analysis suggest that direct instruction is used more often by full-time teachers and in schools that enroll a higher number of students and have a higher teacher workload, that is, more instructional time. While controlling for the type of settlement (city, big or small town, village), the analysis shows no relationship between the frequency of using a direct instruction style and teachers' age, gender, and teaching experience (seniority).

Regarding the equitable distribution of learning styles, our analysis shows that teaching and learning styles are more diverse in schools with students with higher SES, but less diverse in schools with students with lower SES (figure 2.22). The difference for group work and individual work is significant, while direct instruction and team teaching show little difference with regard to student SES.

The student wealth index and student SES show a significant difference in learning outcomes. The difference is equivalent to three-quarters of a standard deviation or three years of schooling (figure 2.23). The gap is significant, and further analysis on larger samples is warranted.

The major finding of this study supports the argument that *innovative teaching styles positively affect student learning outcomes*. Team teaching and group work are positively correlated with the learning outcomes of students (figure 2.24). At the same time, the use of direct instruction and individual work shows no difference in TIMSS scores. The magnitude of the effect on learning outcomes is significant: (a) the use of team teaching adds four points to the TIMMS score, which accounts for around 10 months of learning, and (b) the use of group work adds three points to the TIMSS score, which accounts around 7 months of learning.

While the findings show significant gains from the use of diverse teaching styles, the question of equity remains important. Therefore, the team ran the same

FIGURE 2.22

Share of teachers who regularly (at least two to four times per week) use teaching practices, by student socioeconomic status

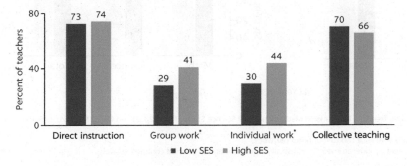

Source: World Bank estimates based on OECD School User Survey (SUS) (OECD 2018) data.
Note: SES = socioeconomic status.
* Statistically significant at 0.1 percent confidence level.

FIGURE 2.23

Student scores, by student wealth index and socioeconomic status index quintiles

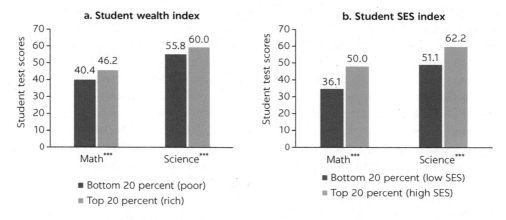

Source: World Bank estimates based on Trends in International Mathematics and Science Study (TIMSS 2019) and OECD School User Survey (SUS) (OECD 2018) data.
Note: SES = socioeconomic status.
*** Statistically significant at 0.01 percent confidence level.

FIGURE 2.24

Student scores, by teaching styles

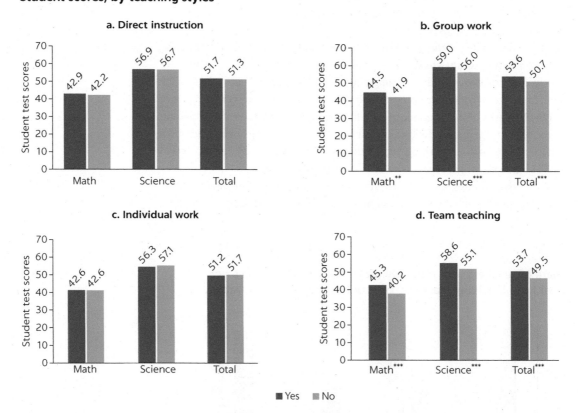

Source: World Bank estimates based on Trends in International Mathematics and Science Study (TIMSS 2019) and OECD School User Survey (SUS) (OECD 2018) data.
Note: A teacher using styles every day or at least two to four times per week.
** Statistically significant at 0.05 percent confidence level; *** Statistically significant at 0.01 percent confidence level.

FIGURE 2.25

Student scores in the bottom 40 percent of socioeconomic status, by teaching style

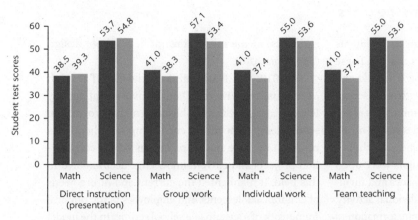

■ Every day or 2–4 times per week   ■ One time per week or less often

Source: World Bank estimates based on Trends in International Mathematics and Science Study (TIMSS 2019) and OECD School User Survey (SUS) (OECD 2018) data.
* Statistically significant at 0.10 confidence level; ** Statistically significant at 0.05 confidence level.

calculations on the bottom 40 percent of the distribution by SES. The bottom 40 percent was chosen to keep the significance of the observations, as the bottom 20 percent would not provide enough discriminative power due to the sample size.

The data suggest that the strength of the effect of the learning environment fades out but persists for team teaching and group work. Individual work is a significant factor for math performance, specifically for the group of students with lower SES (figure 2.25).

DISCUSSION

This study shows that providing a more diverse education leads to better learning outcomes. Teachers support these diverse practices, and the school learning environment may support (and stimulate) such approaches. The study does not promote any particular teaching style. However, it suggests that diversity in teaching styles may enhance learning outcomes.

Ensuring a conducive environment for group work and team teaching in Russian schools may require different spatial arrangements of school settings. Some international examples of taking a unified government approach to innovations in schools are noteworthy (box 2.1). Several products from Denmark's education reform are publicly available and have been translated into Russian.

Drawing from international lessons and research, the following organization of spaces and furniture may support these teaching styles, while its absence could hinder the learning process.

Effective seating arrangements

Group work and team teaching involve more collaboration between students, as well as teachers and students, which leads to intensive communication activities. How the seating is arranged may help to make this communication more effective. The organization of group work can be done in rows, U-shaped seating layouts, circles, or clusters. A cluster is the arrangement of student desks that allows the teacher to

BOX 2.1

Denmark: School design with the users

In 2005 and 2014, Denmark changed the requirements for secondary and primary school environments. These requirements reflected changes in the curricula and teaching methods and extended the length of the school day to accommodate a minimum of 45 minutes of physical activity per day. Danish municipalities started hiring architects to develop new designs for such schools. The main features of these new designs were open and connected spaces, flexibility of spaces and furniture, availability of areas for group, individual activity, and recess (for example, nooks), and transformation of corridors and stairs into active learning environments (Hallström 2014).

From 2009 to 2018, the Danish Government's Quality Foundation allocated DKr 22 billion for state cofinancing of municipal projects, including the construction of schools. The main emphasis was on involving users (pupils, teachers, administrators, parents,

residents) at the initial stage of new school design (Realdania 2010).

In 2010, the National Association of Danish Municipalities and the Danish investment agency Realdania prepared and published a model program on school design. The model curriculum for schools was based on the case studies of various school construction projects and current knowledge accumulated in this field. It highlighted the current and future needs of children, adolescents, and employees in the physical framework of a sustainable school setting. In the model program, particular attention was paid to how different principles of school physical environment can better support important needs for the school's activities. A model program is a catalog of inspiration that can be used actively in planning, programming, construction, design, and daily operation, when the client and users both want to achieve good results (Realdania 2010).

place children either in groups or in pairs. Together with U-shaped seating, it is considered a suitable arrangement of students for cooperative learning (Ridling 1994). According to the research findings, students sitting in circles can engage significantly more during the lesson than students sitting in rows. At the same time, students sitting in cluster settings are more active than students sitting in rows, but less active than those sitting in circles (Rosenfield, Lambert, and Black 1985).

Acoustical arrangements

Intensive communication, which occurs during team teaching and group work, requires special acoustical conditions for speaking and listening. Teachers and students should be able to hear each other clearly over short distances within the class zone, while the zone beyond the class should be free of noise. It is important to maintain an acoustical balance between different learning activity zones, including areas for private communication (Vugts et al. 2017).

Open-plan arrangements

A diversity of activities during group work and team teaching requires the possibility of eliminating spatial barriers within the learning environments and evolving into more open areas. A study on teacher practices and learning environments in Australia and New Zealand reveals that different open-plan arrangements correlate with better scores on deep learning of students and are associated with fewer teacher-centered practices (box 2.2; Imms et al. 2017).

BOX 2.2

Australia: Demand for new layouts

Australia is experiencing a boom in school construction due to the growing number of school-age children (17 percent increase by 2026). Land prices, urban density, and need for cost efficiency have created a new trend in school design in Australia—"vertical" (high-rise) schools. The physical environment of this type of school has the following characteristics:

- High-rise buildings

- Multifunctionality of a facility (school usually includes a preschool, primary, and secondary school under one roof)

- Connection to the local community (some parts of the facility are designed to be open in evening hours to other users such as elderly populations and adults, which guarantees optimal use of the building

- Sharing of some functional spaces with the city (for example, a public library)

- Openness and flexibility of school spaces, both indoor and outdoor (Ernst & Young 2018)

However, the analysis of the Innovative Learning Environments and Teacher Change study found that conventional or traditional classrooms account for about 75 percent of all spaces in Australian and New Zealand schools. Teachers in these environments still use a direct instruction approach to deliver education, and students are less involved in deep learning (Imms et al. 2017).

FIGURE 2.26

A typology of six spatial arrangements found in schools

a. Classrooms along corridors

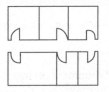

b. Classrooms with a breakout space

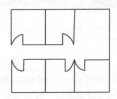

c. Classrooms with flexible walls

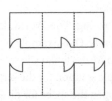

d. Classrooms with flexible walls and breakout space

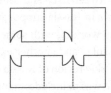

e. Open plan with the possibility of creating classrooms

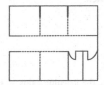

f. Open plan

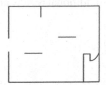

Source: OECD 2019.

FIGURE 2.27

Example of a school in the Russian Federation with an open multifunctional space

Source: © Governor of Yamalo/Nenetsk autonomus Okrug, Russian Federation. Used with the permission of the Governor of Yamalo/Nenetsk autonomus Okrug, Russian Federation. Further permission required for reuse.

The typology of the most common school learning environment arrangements is suggested by the studies of Imms et al. (2017) and the OECD (2019) (figure 2.26, panels a–f). These typologies share a common vision related to the flexibility of different levels between fixed and completely open-plan schools.

Few schools in Russia support these new types of learning. The World Bank team has been working with some of these schools recently. One example is the shiny Horoshkola,[3] and another example is the school in Muravlenko City of the Yamalo-Nenetskiy region of Russia (figure 2.27). The simple solution for the school in Muravlenko was to include an internal courtyard and open the space for diverse teaching and learning experiences. There is more anecdotal evidence, with schools reporting innovative practices and spacial arrangements. This practical implementation requires additional review and collection of case studies.

NOTES

1. Based on the evidence from international large-scale assessments, the learning gains on most national and international tests during one year are equal to between one-quarter and one-third of a standard deviation (Woessmann 2016). Thus, in the TIMSS 2019 pilot the difference of five test scores is equivalent to a learning gap of one year of schooling.

2. SES index components include (a) home ownership of assets and (b) parents' education. Home ownership includes availability of books available at home, availability of a personal computer or tablet, desk a for learning, a separate room, Internet access, a mobile phone, musical instruments (for example, violin, piano), an automobile (one or more), an apartment with four or more rooms, and a dishwasher.

3. For information on Horoshkola, see https://horoshkola.ru/.

REFERENCES

Anderson-Butcher, Dawn, Hal A. Lawson, Aidyn Iachini, Gerald Bean, Paul D. Flaspohler, and Keith Zullig. 2010. "Capacity-Related Innovations Resulting from the Implementation of a Community Collaboration Model for School Improvement." *Journal of Educational and Psychological Consultation* 20 (4): 257–87.

Barrett, Peter, Fay Davies, Yufan Zhang, and Lucinda Barrett. 2015. "The Impact of Classroom Design on Pupils' Learning: Final Results of a Holistic, Multi-Level Analysis." *Building and Environment* 89 (July): 118–33.

Barrett, Peter, Alberto Treves, Tigran Shmis, Diego Ambasz, and Maria Ustinova. 2019. *The Impact of School Infrastructure on Learning: A Synthesis of the Evidence.* International Development in Focus. Washington, DC: World Bank. https://openknowledge.worldbank.org/handle/10986/30920.

Blatchford, Peter, Ed Baines, Christine Rubie-Davies, Paul Bassett, and Anne Chowne. 2006. "The Effect of a New Approach to Group-Work on Pupil-Pupil and Teacher-Pupil Interaction." *Journal of Educational Psychology* 98 (4): 750–65.

Dekker, Rijkje, Marianne Elshout-Mohr, and Terry Wood. 2006. "How Children Regulate Their Own Collaborative Learning." *Educational Studies in Mathematics* 62 (1): 57–79.

Ernst & Young. 2018. "Revolutionizing Education from the Ground up: How Will Vertical Schools Change the Nature of Education?" https://www.ey.com/Publication/vwLUAssets/ey-revolutionising-education-from-ground-up/$FILE/ey-revolutionising-education-from-ground-up-how-will-vertical-schools-change-the-nature-of-education.pdf.

Fielding, Michael. 2006. "Leadership, Radical Collegiality, and the Necessity of Person-Centered Education." Paper presented at the ESRC Teaching and Learning Research Programme (TLRP) Thematic Seminar Series, "Contexts, Communities, Networks: Mobilising Learners' Resources and Relationships in Different Domains," Seminar Four, "Cultures, Values, Identities, and Power," University of Exeter, February 22.

Hallström, Sofia. 2014. "Danish Lessons." *FORM (Nordic magazine on architecture and design)* 5: 84–86.

Imms, Wesley, Marian Mahat, Terry Byers, and Dan Murphy. 2017. *Type and Use of Innovative Learning Environments in Australasian Schools.* ILETC Survey No. 1. Melbourne: LEaRN, University of Melbourne. http://www.iletc.com.au/wp-content/uploads/2017/07/TechnicalReport_Web.pdf.

Oblinger, Diana, and Joan K. Lippincott. 2006. "Learning Spaces." *Brockport Bookshelf* 78, College at Brockport, State University of New York. https://digitalcommons.brockport.edu/bookshelf/78.

OECD (Organisation for Economic Co-operation and Development). 2018. *OECD School User Survey: Improving Learning Space Together.* http://www.oecd.org/education/OECD-School-User-Survey-2018.pdf.

———. 2019. "Analytical Framework for Case Study Collection: Effective Learning Environments." EDU/EDPC/GNEELE(2018)3/REV1, Group of National Experts on Effective Learning Environments, Directorate for Education and Skills, Education Policy Committee, OECD, Paris. https://bit.ly/2MLS9I6.

Realdania. 2010. "МОДЕЛЬНАЯ ПРОГРАММА ДЛЯ ОБЩЕОБРАЗОВАТЕЛЬНЫХ ШКОЛАгентство [Danish Model Program for Schools]." Realdania, Copenhagen. http://documents.worldbank.org/curated/en/734251533070308219/pdf/Danish-Modelprogram-for-Schools-RUS.pdf.

Ridling, Zaine. 1994. "The Effects of Three Seating Arrangements on Teachers' Use of Selective Interactive Verbal Behaviors." Paper presented at the Annual Meeting of the American Educational Research Association, New Orleans, LA, April 4–8.

Rosenfield, Peter, Nadine M. Lambert, and Allen Black. 1985. "Desk Arrangement Effects on Pupil Classroom Behavior." *Journal of Educational Psychology* 77 (1): 101–08. http://dx.doi.org/10.1037/0022-0663.77.1.101.

TIMSS (Trends in Mathematics and Science Study). 2019. Retrieved at: http://www.centeroko.ru/timss19/timss2019_info.html.

Vugts, Jeroen, Esther van Oorschot-Slaat, Collin Campbell, and Holger Brokmann. 2017. "Effective Open Learning Landscapes and the Well-Being of Teachers and Students." Paper prepared for the 12th ICBEN (International Commission on Biological Effects of Noise) Congress on Noise as a Public Health Problem, Zurich, June 18–22.

Woessmann, Ludger. 2016. "The Importance of School Systems: Evidence from International Differences in Student Achievement." *Journal of Economic Perspectives* 30 (3): 3–31.

World Bank. 2018. "Education Equity in the Russian Federation: Summary Report." Working Paper 127743, World Bank, Washington, DC. http://documents.worldbank.org/curated/en/139291530189329351/Education-Equity-in-the-Russian-Federation-Summary-Report.

3 Recommendations and Conclusion

RECOMMENDATIONS FOR POLICY MAKERS

This report has examined the situation in Russian schools and education approaches used in classrooms. The main findings confirm the prevalence of traditional practices in Russian schools and the lack of diverse approaches to teaching and learning. Where they exist, diverse practices help to improve student outcomes. In terms of the framework, the study shows that the basic needs of Russian education are covered, apart from security and bullying. The spaces in schools are not always optimal for learning, and there are areas for policy attention to improve schools further for teachers and students. The fit for purpose is not matched for those schools that try to innovate with learning. Thus, to improve learning environments and learning outcomes, significant upgrades will need to be made.

The research suggests three pillars for policy makers to consider.

Pillar 1. Nationwide school infrastructure analysis and development

- *The existing stock of school buildings needs to be reviewed and documented.* The characteristics to be documented include the current conditions, types of designs, cost of maintenance, and need for rehabilitation.

- *The majority of Russian schools feature traditional corridors that are not conducive to flexible educational approaches.* Teachers in Russian schools have the ability to change layouts and arrangements within classrooms. However, the design of corridors and classrooms and lack of larger common spaces in most schools limit the use of team teaching. The organization of small group work in breakout rooms may also be limited. The study suggests that school learning spaces are not limited to the classroom and that all school spaces should be used for learning. Simple solutions informed by the best practices and modern architecture may be applied at scale in the Russian Federation (boxes 2.1 and 2.2).

Pillar 2. School leadership

- *Targeted efforts are needed.* The study shows that advanced teaching styles are frequently used in schools with a large concentration of students with higher socioeconomic status. These teaching practices work well regardless of the student's socioeconomic status (SES). It is thus recommended to build policies that encourage schools to use these approaches. Specifically, the analysis shows that the arrangements for individual learning can improve the learning outcomes of students with lower SES.

- *Bullying is a problem in Russian schools, and it is both an issue of safety and an issue of learning outcomes.* The study clearly shows that bullying by itself is a complicated phenomenon with several dimensions related both to gender and to equity. Most important, a higher frequency of bullying is negatively correlated with lower academic achievement. Bullying more often occurs in schools with a concentration of students with low SES and, at the same time, is associated with lower Trends in Mathematics and Science Study (TIMSS) results. Conducting more research in this area and devising measures to combat bullying—both by developing psychological resilience and by creating safer learning spaces—should be considered. Transparency in schools and open areas may help to reduce bullying (passive measures). Creating spaces that could limit the possibility of bullying is a new area of research and experimentation that could be promoted in Russia.

- *School satisfaction has a direct link to academic achievements and teacher job satisfaction.* Better learning spaces in schools lead to better satisfaction of teachers with their job and their workplace. This is an area of agreement between teachers and principals. The satisfaction of students with schools has a positive connection with their academic achievement. Thus, creating better schools leads to better teaching and better learning. The government may consider several suggestions offered here for designing policy documents and functional requirements for new and existing schools in Russia.

Pillar 3. Analysis and improvement of classroom practices

- *An understanding of teaching and learning in classroom settings in Russia needs to be expanded.* Similar to the findings of the World Bank equity study in 2018, this review sheds light on the emerging practices (World Bank 2018). For example, while schools and teachers in Russia claim that they use team teaching and other best practices, they do so rarely. While teachers in Norway say that they use layouts supporting team teaching either every day in 50 percent of the cases or at least once a week in all other cases, Russian teachers say that they never arrange such activities in 68 percent of the cases. The research and identification of these practices in Russian schools may yield valuable lessons for other schools and the system overall.

- *A strong relationship exists between the academic achievement of students and teaching styles.* The most advantageous teaching styles for learning outcomes are those where teachers organize group work for the students and where teachers work in team-teaching arrangements. As reflected in the TIMSS results, there is a difference of roughly one year of learning between those students who are exposed to such approaches and those who are not. This finding should lead policy makers to pay more attention to teacher training and preservice and in-service institutions to incorporate the practice of team teaching into their training.

CONCLUSION

This study is the first of its kind to suggest a connection between learning environments and learning outcomes as measured by TIMSS. The study sheds more light on the initial research questions and, for the sampled schools, shows that how teaching and learning are delivered matters. When teachers arrange group work in the classroom and work collaboratively with large groups of students, they achieve learning gains for all income groups.

The perception of schools by students, their feeling of security, and the frequency of bullying have a direct connection with learning outcomes. Better conditions in schools and rare to no bullying have a strong link with positive learning outcomes. The study shows that solving some of the problems (like severe bullying) could help to close a one-year learning gap. Therefore, smart investments in learning environments and teacher preparation can help to improve national education and competitiveness.

This study has potential limitations. The sample size includes mostly urban schools from three Russian regions, located in the central and northwest administrative districts of the country. A larger sample, consisting of all regions, would yield statistically more significant results. Additionally, it would be essential to include more rural schools as well as different types of schools (for example, private, specialized) and to analyze potential disparities between the territorial areas and the regions themselves.

The lack of empirical research on learning environments in Russia requires more in-depth studies on the practices of teachers and students in existing learning environments. Case studies, focus groups, and interviews with survey respondents could bring additional qualitative information to the research findings. It is especially important to expand the knowledge base on the practice of team teaching, which seems to be a promising approach to the delivery of learning.

Lastly, further study should include several measures of socioemotional skills or collaborative problem-solving skills, the 21st-century skills that seem to be better developed in innovative settings.

REFERENCE

World Bank. 2018. "Education Equity in the Russian Federation: Summary Report." Working Paper 127743, World Bank, Washington, DC. http://documents.worldbank.org/curated /en/139291530189329351/Education-Equity-in-the-Russian-Federation-Summary-report.